BEIRUT
VACATION GUIDE
2023

The Essential and Ultimate Guide to Beirut's Hotels, Cuisines, Shopping Tips, Insider's Tips, Top Attractions, History, and Culture

ALFRED FLORES

Copyright © 2023, Alfred Flores

TABLE OF CONTENTS

INTRODUCTION

Welcome to the "Beirut Vacation Guide 2023"! Whether you're a seasoned traveler or embarking on your first adventure, we invite you to immerse yourself in the vibrant and captivating city of Beirut. Nestled along the mesmerizing Mediterranean coastline, Beirut is a city that resonates with history, culture, and an undeniable spirit that continues to thrive despite the challenges it has faced.

Why Visit Beirut?

Beirut, the beating heart of Lebanon, is a city like no other, offering a mesmerizing blend of ancient heritage and modern charm. This bustling metropolis boasts a rich tapestry of cultural influences, from its Phoenician roots to its Ottoman and French colonial past, resulting in a unique fusion of traditions that can be felt throughout its streets, architecture, and cuisine. From the bustling souks filled with aromatic spices and colorful textiles to the vibrant nightlife and art scene, Beirut has something to offer every type of traveler.

However, Beirut's allure goes beyond its cultural richness. The city's picturesque landscapes, framed by the Mediterranean Sea and the breathtaking Lebanese mountains, create an atmosphere of natural beauty that captivates visitors year-round. The warm and welcoming nature of the Lebanese people adds a special touch to the experience, making it feel like a home away from home.

How to Use This Guide:

In this comprehensive "Beirut Vacation Guide 2023," we have meticulously curated a collection of the city's most captivating attractions, hidden gems, and practical information to help you make the most of your visit. Whether you're seeking historical landmarks, culinary delights, scenic spots, or lively entertainment, this guide has you covered.

Each section is thoughtfully designed to cater to your specific interests and preferences, allowing you to craft a personalized itinerary that ensures your Beirut experience is nothing short of extraordinary. From solo travelers seeking adventure to families looking for enriching experiences and couples seeking a romantic getaway, this guide aims to be your trusted companion throughout your journey.

Beirut: Quick Facts and Statistics:

- Capital City: Beirut is the capital and largest city of Lebanon, located along the country's Mediterranean coastline.

- Historical Significance: Beirut has a rich history dating back thousands of years, with evidence of human settlement found in archaeological sites dating to the Bronze Age.

- Language: The official language of Beirut is Arabic, while French and English are widely spoken and used in business and education.

- Religious Diversity: Beirut is known for its religious diversity, with various religious communities coexisting, including Christians, Muslims, and others.

- Post-Civil War Rebuilding: Following the Lebanese Civil War (1975-1990), Beirut underwent extensive reconstruction, resulting in a modern cityscape alongside remnants of historical architecture.

- Cultural Hub: Beirut has a vibrant arts and cultural scene, with numerous museums, galleries, theaters, and music venues showcasing both traditional and contemporary works.

- Economic Center: The city serves as Lebanon's economic and financial center, with a significant role in the region's banking and commerce.

- Higher Education: Beirut is home to prestigious universities, including the American University of Beirut (AUB) and Université Saint-Joseph (USJ), contributing to its reputation as an educational hub.

- Mediterranean Climate: The city enjoys a Mediterranean climate, characterized by hot and humid summers and mild, rainy winters.

- Population: As of September 2021, Beirut had an estimated population of around 2.4 million in the metropolitan area.
- Time Zone: Beirut operates on Eastern European Time (EET), which is UTC+2, and Eastern European Summer Time (EEST), which is UTC+3 during daylight saving time.

- Economy: Beirut's economy is diverse, with sectors including banking, finance, trade, tourism, and services. Historically, Lebanon has been considered a regional banking and financial hub. However, the country has faced economic challenges, including high public debt and inflation.

Throughout this guide, we will delve deeper into the city's rich history, provide practical tips on getting around, showcase the best places to savor the local cuisine, and introduce you to the warm hospitality that defines Beirut.

So, whether you're planning your first visit to this remarkable city or looking to rediscover its timeless charm, let the "Beirut Vacation Guide 2023" be your compass, guiding you through an unforgettable journey in the enchanting realm of

Beirut. Let's embark on this adventure together and uncover the magic that awaits in the heart of Lebanon's capital city.

CHAPTER ONE:
Getting to Know Beirut

Beirut, the captivating capital of Lebanon, beckons travelers with its intriguing mix of history, culture, and natural beauty. Nestled on the eastern shore of the Mediterranean Sea, this ancient city has been a cultural crossroads for millennia, witnessing the rise and fall of empires, and now stands as a vibrant metropolis that exudes an unmistakable charm. In this chapter, we will delve into the geographical overview, climate and weather, history and culture, as well as the festivals and events that make Beirut an exceptional destination.

Geographical Overview

Beirut is located in the western part of Lebanon, bordered by the Mediterranean Sea to the west. Since ancient times, it has served as a crucial junction for both maritime and land-based commerce routes due to its location at the middle of Lebanon's coastline. Due to its advantageous location as a crossroads of Europe, Asia, and Africa, the city has a rich cultural heritage and a significant historical background.

Beirut is nestled between the sea and the scenic Lebanese Mountains, providing a picturesque backdrop for the city. The nearby mountains offer excellent opportunities for outdoor enthusiasts, with hiking trails, charming villages, and stunning vistas waiting to be explored. Meanwhile, the coastline boasts beautiful beaches and promenades, where locals and visitors alike enjoy leisurely strolls and refreshing dips in the Mediterranean waters.

Climate and Weather

Beirut experiences a Mediterranean climate, characterized by hot and dry summers and mild, rainy winters. The city enjoys around 300 days of sunshine annually, making it an ideal destination for year-round visits. The summer months, from June to September, bring warm temperatures, with averages ranging from 25°C to 30°C (77°F to 86°F). It is the peak tourist season when the city comes alive with festivals, outdoor concerts, and bustling beach life.

Winter brings colder temperatures, with averages ranging from 13°C to 18°C (55°F to 64°F) from

December to February. Snowfall on the mountains surrounding Beirut is normal during this time of year, but it is rare in the city itself. With their warmer temperatures, spring (March to May) and fall (October to November) are great times to visit the city's attractions without the summertime throngs.

History and Culture

With more than 5,000 years of history, Beirut is among the world's oldest continuously inhabited cities. Originally called Berytus, it was a Phoenician settlement. Over the ages, it was dominated by a number of civilizations, including the Romans, Byzantines, Arabs, Crusaders, Ottomans, and French, all of whom left their profound cultural imprints on the city.

In recent memory, the Lebanese Civil War, which raged from 1975 to 1990, presented Beirut with many difficulties. Notwithstanding the effects of the conflict, the city has shown incredible fortitude and has subsequently come to represent optimism and rebirth.

Beirut is a thriving cultural melting pot where the ancient and the new coexist together in the modern era. It is a deeply embedded part of the local culture to extend a warm welcome to guests who come to enjoy the city's gastronomic delights as well as its rich heritage and customs. Known for its robust flavors and fresh ingredients, Lebanese food is a must-try while here.

Festivals and Events

The calendar of events in Beirut is jam-packed with colorful festivals and celebrations of the city's rich cultural legacy. There's always something going on in Beirut's streets, be it music and dance, art, food, or religious events.

Every year in October, one of the most eagerly awaited occasions is the Beirut International Film Festival. Filmmakers, actors, and moviegoers from all over the world come to this esteemed event to celebrate and exhibit the craft of filmmaking.

World Music Day, or Fête de la Musique, is an annual June event that turns the city into a vibrant stage for performances by musicians of all genres in the parks, squares, and streets. This joyful music and celebration day captures the spirit of the city's love of the arts and creative expression.

In Beirut, religious holidays are quite important to the local culture. For Muslims, Ramadan is a holy month that creates a unique ambience in the city with its vibrant decorations, lively parties, and mouthwatering traditional feasts given during Iftar, the breaking of the fast at dusk. The celebration of Eid al-Fitr, which commemorates the conclusion of Ramadan, is a time for happiness and giving as friends and family gather to share presents and greetings.

Beirut also celebrates Christmas in style, with the streets twinkling with bright lights that create a mystical ambiance. The city comes alive with music, activities, and festivities that bring its communities together as many Christian denominations honor the day.

In summary, Beirut captivates the hearts of everyone who visits with its intriguing geographic location, varied climate, rich history, and dynamic culture. Beirut is a living example of the tenacity and passion of its people, both in its historical legacy and its allure today. Its calendar of festivals and events imbues each visit with a distinct and unforgettable quality. The beauty, friendliness, and infinite energy of Beirut will charm you as you set out on your adventure to discover this remarkable city.

CHAPTER TWO:
Planning Your Trip to Beirut

Beirut, with its rich history, vibrant culture, and stunning landscapes, is a captivating destination that appeals to a wide range of travelers. When planning a trip to Beirut, you should consider the best time to visit, visa and travel requirements, transportation options, accommodation choices, and the importance of travel insurance. This chapter provides a comprehensive guide to help you plan an unforgettable journey to the enchanting city of Beirut.

Best Time to Visit

Beirut experiences a Mediterranean climate, characterized by hot and dry summers and mild and rainy winters. The best time to visit Beirut is during the spring (April to June) and autumn (September to November) seasons when the weather is pleasant, and the city comes alive with festivals and cultural events.

Springtime brings pleasant weather, blossoming flowers, and the opportunity to take in the customs of Lebanese Easter celebrations. With its lower temperatures, autumn is a great time to see historical places and engage in outdoor activities without the oppressive summer heat.

Summer travel is very popular, especially for those who enjoy the beach (June to August). On the other hand, there is a chance of extreme heat waves and tourist congestion in the city. If you want to go in the summer, pack for the heat and think about lodging close to the ocean so you can take advantage of the cool sea air.

Winter, which lasts from December through February, is Beirut's low season because of the cold, wet weather. Even if the city might not be at its finest at this time of year, it still offers cheap tourists a great chance to see the city without the crowds and save money on lodging.

Visa and Travel Requirements

It is crucial to confirm the visa and travel restrictions specific to your country before making travel arrangements to Beirut. Certain nationals of other countries are exempt from needing a visa to enter Lebanon; however, others may need to obtain one from the Lebanese embassy or consulate in their place of residence.

Visas are available for purchase upon arrival for stays up to ninety days for nationals of the

European Union, the United States, Canada, Australia, and many Arab nations. It is advisable to confirm that you have the appropriate papers for your visit, though, by contacting the closest Lebanese embassy or consulate.

Make sure your passport is valid for a minimum of six months after the day you intend to leave Lebanon. Additionally, at the time of your travel, find out if there are any health-related restrictions or any special entry procedures because of COVID-19.

How to Get There

The main gateway into the city is Beirut-Rafic Hariri International Airport (BEY), which has excellent connections to a number of foreign locations. Numerous airlines provide direct flights from major cities in North America, Europe, the Middle East, and Asia to Beirut.

You can select from a wide range of airlines, including Middle Eastern carriers like Middle East Airlines (MEA), Emirates, Qatar Airways, and Turkish Airlines, depending on your location and budget. discount-conscious flights are also available to European travelers on discount airlines like Ryanair and Wizz Air.

Getting Around

Due to its small size, Beirut is a pleasant city to explore on foot, particularly in neighborhoods like Downtown, Gemmayze, and Hamra. But if you want to travel farther or see places outside of the city center, you have a few options for getting around:

a) Taxis: Using a taxi to go around Beirut is convenient. Before beginning the ride, make sure to haggle over the price or request that the driver utilize the meter.

b) Ride-Hailing Apps: Uber and Careem are available in Beirut and provide a dependable and secure substitute for conventional taxis.

c) Public Transportation: Buses connect important neighborhoods, and services run on defined routes for a fixed charge. Beirut's public transportation system consists of shared taxis, also referred to as "service" or "van."

d) Car Rental: Hiring a car is a possibility if you want to travel outside of Beirut. However, the city can have chaotic traffic, and parking can be difficult, so this choice is best suited for visitors who are accustomed to maneuvering through congested metropolitan streets.

Accommodation Options

Beirut offers a diverse range of accommodation options to suit every traveler's preferences and budget. From luxurious hotels with breathtaking views to charming boutique stays and budget-friendly hostels, there is something for everyone. Below are real samples of accommodation options in Beirut:

Luxury Hotels:

a) Four Seasons Hotel Beirut: Located in the heart of Downtown Beirut, the Four Seasons offers elegant rooms and suites with panoramic views of the Mediterranean Sea. The hotel features world-class dining, a rooftop pool, and a luxurious spa.

b) Le Gray Beirut: Situated in the vibrant neighborhood of Martyrs' Square, Le Gray is a contemporary boutique hotel with stylish rooms and a rooftop pool. The hotel's Indigo on the Roof restaurant offers panoramic views of the city.

Mid-Range Hotels :

a) Saifi Urban Gardens: The trendy Saifi Village is home to the boutique hotel Saifi Urban Gardens, which provides cozy accommodations with contemporary conveniences. A serene haven in the middle of the city is the hotel's garden courtyard.

b) The Smallville Hotel: The lively Badaro area is home to The Smallville Hotel, which has modern accommodations and a rooftop bar with breathtaking views of Beirut.

Budget Hotels:
a) Minto Suites: located in Hamra, Minto Suites is a great choice for tourists on a tight budget because it provides reasonably priced, well-equipped apartments with kitchenettes.

b) Napoleon Hotel: This reasonably priced hotel is close to Beirut's National Museum and offers simple rooms with all the conveniences you need.

Travel Insurance

Travel insurance is a crucial aspect of trip planning that provides financial protection in case of unforeseen events such as trip cancellations, flight delays, medical emergencies, or lost luggage. It is highly recommended to purchase comprehensive travel insurance before embarking on your journey to Beirut.

Make sure the destinations and activities you intend to partake in during your vacation are covered by your travel insurance. Make sure your insurance policy covers activities like adventure sports and outdoor activities, for instance, if you intend to engage in them.

Carefully review the insurance policy's terms and conditions, and ask the insurance company any questions you may have. Throughout your vacation, make sure you have a copy of your insurance policy and the emergency contact details with you.

In conclusion, planning your trip to Beirut requires careful consideration of the best time to visit, visa and travel requirements, transportation options, accommodation choices, and the importance of travel insurance. By ensuring that you have all the necessary documents, securing reliable transportation, choosing suitable accommodation, and having comprehensive travel insurance, you can embark on a seamless and unforgettable journey to this captivating city. Whether you are exploring the historical sites, savoring the delectable cuisine, or immersing yourself in the vibrant culture, Beirut promises to leave a lasting impression on your heart and mind.

CHAPTER THREE:
Exploring Beirut's Neighborhoods

The vibrant capital of Lebanon, Beirut, captivates tourists with its varied neighborhoods, each of which offers a special fusion of modernity, culture, and history. Discover the unique attraction of each area, whether it's the vibrant streets of Downtown Beirut, the artistic allure of Gemmayze and Mar Mikhael, or the cultural diversity of Achrafieh. Come along for a tour of some of the most interesting places of Beirut, including Downtown, Gemmayze and Mar Mikhael, Hamra District, Achrafieh, and the charming Corniche and Raouche neighborhoods.

Downtown Beirut

Downtown Beirut, often referred to as "Solidere," is the commercial and historical center of the city. After the Lebanese Civil War, it underwent extensive reconstruction, and it is now a prime example of urban rebirth. The region's flawlessly restored Ottoman and French colonial architecture seamlessly combines the old and the new.

It is a popular site for dining and shopping because of the variety of posh boutiques, fine dining establishments, and chic cafes you will come across as you stroll along the lovely streets. Situated between old buildings and adorned with a clock tower, Nejmeh Square is a prominent landmark in the neighborhood. The Beirut Souks, a contemporary retail center that honors historic Lebanese souks and offers a wide range of products from regional handicrafts to luxury brands from around the world, is a feature of Downtown Beirut.

Gemmayze and Mar Mikhael

Gemmayze and Mar Mikhael are adjacent neighborhoods that have a bohemian vibe and are popular with young creatives, trend-setters, and art enthusiasts. There are lots of trendy cafes, pubs, and art galleries in Mar Mikhael, but Gemmayze is known for its little streets covered in vibrant graffiti.

Once the sun sets, these neighborhoods come alive and become bustling centers of nightlife. By visiting the many art galleries exhibiting the creations of regional and worldwide artists, you may fully immerse yourself in the city's current art scene. Apart from that, Mar Mikhael is a foodie paradise with a wide array of eateries and street food carts selling delicious Lebanese and other cuisines.

Hamra District

The Hamra District is a vibrant, active neighborhood with a rich history and cultural value, situated between the Mediterranean Sea and the Lebanese Mountains. It served as the city's cultural center in the middle of the 20th century and was well-known for its theaters, bookstores, and intellectual events.

Even now, Hamra is still a popular neighborhood with a diverse population of visitors, locals, and students. The neighborhood, which is full of stores, cafes, and eateries, is still a hub for academic debate because it is home to numerous colleges and cultural organizations. The American University of Beirut (AUB), a prominent figure in Lebanon's academic and cultural environment, is a must-see monument in Hamra. It boasts an amazing campus.

Achrafieh

Achrafieh is a posh residential neighborhood of historical significance that is known for its magnificent architecture, lively community, and quaint little streets. This area skillfully blends the energy of the present with the nostalgia of the past. Several sectors, each with a unique personality, make up Achrafieh.

The Sassine Square neighborhood is well-known for its fine dining establishments, boutiques, and fashionable cafes. It's also a great place to shop. In the meanwhile, the magnificent estate that serves as the Sursock Museum is home to an amazing collection of modern and contemporary art, providing visitors with a fascinating cultural experience.

Corniche and Raouche

Beirut's Corniche is a scenic coastal promenade that stretches along the Mediterranean Sea, offering breathtaking views of the azure waters and the iconic Pigeon Rocks of Raouche. The Corniche is a favorite spot for locals and tourists alike to take leisurely walks, jog, or simply enjoy the sea breeze while savoring the beauty of the coastline.

Raouche, situated at the western end of the Corniche, is home to the famous Pigeon Rocks, massive rock formations that rise dramatically from the sea. These geological wonders are a symbol of Beirut and are especially mesmerizing during sunset, when their silhouette against the horizon creates a picture-perfect view.

In conclusion, exploring Beirut's diverse neighborhoods is like embarking on a fascinating journey through time and culture. Every neighborhood has a distinct personality that entices guests to engage in a unique experience of the city's modernism, innovation, and history. Beirut's neighborhoods promise an amazing journey full of fascinating discoveries and treasured memories, from the sophisticated streets of Downtown to the bohemian charm of Gemmayze and Mar Mikhael, the intellectual atmosphere of Hamra, the cultural richness of Achrafieh, and the picturesque Corniche and Raouche.

CHAPTER FOUR:
Top Attractions and Landmarks in Beirut

Beirut, a city steeped in history and culture, boasts a plethora of captivating attractions and landmarks that reflect its rich heritage and dynamic spirit. Every location, from historic ruins to cutting-edge architectural marvels, offers a different perspective on Beirut's history and present. This chapter will cover some of the must-see sites and landmarks in the enchanted city of Beirut, including the National Museum of Beirut, Pigeon Rocks (Raouche), Mohammad Al-Amin Mosque, Martyrs' Square, and the Roman Baths.

National Museum of Beirut

The National Museum of Beirut is a treasure mine of archaeological marvels as well as the guardian of Lebanon's cultural legacy. The museum, which is centrally located in Beirut, is a must-visit location for history buffs and those attempting to solve the enigmas surrounding Lebanon's distant past.

The magnificent collection of objects on display at the museum covers over 5,000 years of history and includes items from many of the civilizations that formerly flourished in the area, such as the Ottomans, Romans, Greeks, and Phoenicians. Immersion in a diverse range of displays is possible for visitors, ranging from elaborate mosaics and statues to prehistoric pottery and artifacts that offer insight into these ancient people' everyday existence.

The sarcophagi hall, which showcases an amazing collection of Phoenician sarcophagus with beautiful stone carvings, is one of the museum's attractions. The "Byblos Collection," a collection of Phoenician gilded bronze figurines, is another well-known exhibit that provides a unique window into the artistic ability of this ancient society.

Pigeon Rocks (Raouche)

Pigeon Rocks, sometimes called Raouche Rocks, are recognizable natural monuments that are considered to be part of Beirut's gorgeous shoreline. They are located on the western fringe of the city. These breathtaking limestone cliffs form a magnificent background for the city's skyline, standing magnificently in the Mediterranean Sea.

The rocks are named after the numerous pigeons that once inhabited the area. A popular way to experience these geological wonders is through a boat tour, where visitors can sail around the rocks and marvel at their grandeur up close. Additionally, Pigeon Rocks are especially captivating during sunset, when the golden hues of the setting sun paint the rocks in a mesmerizing palette of colors.

Mohammad Al-Amin Mosque

Located in Downtown Beirut, the Mohammad Al-Amin Mosque, also referred to as the Blue Mosque, is one of the most notable religious buildings in the city and a spectacular example of Islamic architecture. The mosque bears the name of Sheikh Mohammad Al-Amin, a prominent Sunni Muslim figure in Lebanon who passed away in 2008.

Magnificent domes, elaborate mosaics, and tall minarets are only a few of the mosque's striking Ottoman and Islamic architectural elements. Inside, a roomy prayer hall with magnificent marble flooring and elaborate chandeliers creates a peaceful, serene environment.

The mosque's central location in Downtown Beirut adds to its significance as a place of spiritual and cultural importance, drawing visitors and worshippers alike to admire its beauty and immerse themselves in Lebanon's Islamic heritage.

Martyrs' Square

Al Burj Square, also known as Martyrs' Square, is very significant historically in Beirut and has seen several significant turning points in the history of Lebanon. Located in the heart of Downtown Beirut, the square represents the tenacity and fight for freedom and independence of the city as well as being a major gathering place for residents.

The area has the name of the Lebanese nationalists who were put to death by the Ottoman rulers during World War I. Over time, it has served as a venue for a number of social and political protests, emerging as a hub for the voice and desires of the Lebanese people.

The enormous bronze statue of "The Unknown Soldier," which honors those who gave their lives in defense of Lebanon's freedom, is one of the many historical structures and sites that encircle Martyrs' Square. Due to its prominent location, the square is a must-visit place for history buffs who want to learn about the resilience and spirit of the Lebanese people.

Roman Baths

The Roman Baths in Beirut are evidence of the city's prehistoric heritage and its importance throughout the Roman Empire. These well preserved ruins, which are located in the center of Downtown Beirut, provide an enthralling look into the city's past as a thriving Roman colony.

An extensive complex that functioned as a social and cultural hub for the Roman residents of Berytus, as Beirut was known at the time, included the Roman Baths, which date back to the second century AD. The baths had different areas for socializing and relaxing, as well as hot and cold rooms and swimming pools.

Today, visitors can explore the excavated ruins and imagine the grandeur of this ancient complex. The site is complemented by informative panels that provide historical context, making it an enriching experience for history enthusiasts and anyone eager to connect with Beirut's past.

In conclusion, Beirut's top attractions and landmarks offer an immersive journey through time and culture, providing a diverse array of experiences for every visitor. From the National Museum of Beirut's archaeological wonders to the natural beauty of Pigeon Rocks, the architectural magnificence of Mohammad Al-Amin Mosque, the historical significance of Martyrs' Square, and the Roman Baths' ancient ruins, each site adds a layer of depth to Beirut's allure. As you explore these iconic destinations, you'll gain a deeper appreciation for the city's vibrant past and its enduring spirit, making your visit to Beirut an unforgettable and enriching experience.

CHAPTER FIVE:
Beirut's Culinary Delights

Renowned for its lively culture and extensive history, Beirut is also a great place for foodies looking to explore new flavors. Strong flavors, fresh ingredients, and delectable dishes characterize Lebanese cuisine, which has won praise from all over the world and is a vital component of Beirut's identity. This chapter delves into Beirut's gastronomic offerings, encompassing classic Lebanese dishes, street food and food markets, elegant dining establishments and Lebanese restaurants, the mouthwatering mezze and hummus, and the exquisite Lebanese sweets and desserts that linger on every traveler's palate.

Traditional Lebanese Cuisine

The delicious blend of flavors found in Lebanese cuisine reflects the historical and cultural variety of the nation. The cuisine makes extensive use of lean proteins, aromatic herbs, fresh vegetables, and olive oil to produce tasty and healthful dishes. Chickpeas, lentils, eggplants, tomatoes, cucumbers, and a variety of herbs like parsley, mint, and thyme are typical components.

Recipes such as Tabbouleh, a cool salad with chopped parsley, mint, tomatoes, onions, bulgur wheat, and lemon juice and olive oil, are a clear reflection of the Mediterranean influence. Smashed pita bread, mixed greens, tomatoes, cucumbers, sumac, and acidic dressing combine to make the colorful salad known as fattoush, which is another renowned meal.

Grilled meats and kebabs are staples of Lebanese cuisine. The delectable aromas and soft textures of these dishes—whether they are juicy Kofta (spiced ground meat skewers), luscious Shish Taouk (marinated chicken skewers), or tender lamb chops—are highly praised.

Street Food and Food Markets

Beirut's streets come alive with an array of enticing street food options, providing a culinary experience that is as authentic as it is delicious. Fava beans or ground chickpeas combined with spices and herbs to make falafel, a popular vegetarian meal, is a must-try street snack in Beirut. A common accompaniment to pita bread are these crunchy, golden-brown balls, pickles, and tahini sauce.

Another common street meal is manakish. Sometimes called "Lebanese pizza," it's just flatbread with minced meat, cheese, or za'atar, a mixture of herbs and spices. Around the city, bakeries and street vendors serve manakish, a well-liked breakfast choice.

Taste Jallab, a traditional Lebanese beverage poured over crushed ice and made with grape molasses, rose water, and pine nuts, for a pleasant and refreshing treat. On a hot day, it's the ideal option to satisfy your thirst.

When it comes to food markets, Souk el Tayeb, located in Beirut's Martyrs' Square, is a must-visit. This farmers' market offers a wonderful opportunity to sample a wide variety of local produce, artisanal goods, and freshly prepared foods. From homemade jams and preserves to aromatic spices and freshly baked bread, the market is a sensory delight that showcases the bounty of Lebanon's fertile lands.

Fine Dining and Lebanese Restaurants

There are several excellent eating establishments in Beirut that take Lebanese food to a new level of culinary mastery. These restaurants maintain the authenticity of traditional Lebanese tastes while providing a more upscale dining experience.

Many of Beirut's fine dining establishments create inventive dishes that defy conventional recipes by honoring regional ingredients and seasonal freshness. These eateries frequently serve contemporary takes on traditional

Lebanese fare, combining regional influences and techniques from around the world of cooking.

Some fine dining establishments even incorporate elements of molecular gastronomy to present dishes in creative and visually stunning ways, making the dining experience a feast for the eyes as well as the palate.

Mezze and Hummus

Mezze is a staple of Lebanese cuisine and represents the concept of sharing and group dining. Enjoy a delicious assortment of flavors and textures that entice the taste senses with these small appetizers, served prior to the main course.

Hummus, a creamy blend of chickpeas, tahini, lemon juice, and garlic, is a star in the world of mezze. It is often served as a dip with warm pita bread and garnished with a drizzle of olive oil and a sprinkle of sumac. Hummus is a staple on the Lebanese dining table and is enjoyed as a versatile accompaniment to various dishes.

In addition to hummus, mezze may include dishes such as Baba Ghanoush (smoky roasted eggplant dip), Tabbouleh, Moutabal (eggplant dip), Warak Enab (stuffed grape leaves), and Kibbeh (deep-fried or baked bulgur and minced meat patties), among others. The combination of flavors and textures in mezze ensures a delightful and satisfying dining experience.

Lebanese Sweets and Desserts

Sweets from Lebanon are a reflection of the nation's enjoyment of complex flavors, soft textures, and decadent desserts. Havarla, a popular dessert in Beirut and the Middle East, is a pastry consisting of layers of thin filo dough filled with chopped nuts, sweetened with syrup or honey, and scented with cinnamon.

Another popular sweet is Knafeh, a luscious dessert made with shredded phyllo dough layered with sweetened cheese or semolina, and topped with a rose or orange blossom flavored syrup. It is often garnished with crushed pistachios for added texture and visual appeal.

For those with a penchant for floral flavors, Rosewater or Orange Blossom water-infused sweets are a must-try. These floral essences are used to flavor many traditional Lebanese desserts, including Maamoul (shortbread cookies filled with dates or nuts), Atayef (stuffed pancakes), and Ashta (clotted cream).

In conclusion, a wide range of tastes and preferences can be satisfied by the gastronomic adventure that Beirut's culinary pleasures provide. Every culinary experience in Beirut is a celebration of the nation's culinary heritage, from the rich flavors of traditional Lebanese cuisine to the enticing street food and food markets, the artistry of fine dining restaurants, the joy of sharing mezze and hummus, and the indulgence of Lebanese sweets and desserts. A trip to Beirut is an invitation to indulge in the many flavors of this captivating city, leaving guests with a memorable experience and a need to come back for more delectable culinary explorations.

CHAPTER SIX:
Nightlife and Entertainment in Beirut

As the sun sets, Beirut, the energetic capital of Lebanon, changes into a colorful and energetic cityscape with a varied and fascinating nightlife to suit every taste and inclination. Beirut offers an incredible nightlife and entertainment scene, ranging from chic pubs and energetic nightclubs to engaging live music venues and cultural events. In order to make sure that guests have an incredibly amazing and exciting night in the center of this fascinating city, we will delve into the many aspects of Beirut's after-dark offerings in this chapter. These include its bars and pubs, nightclubs and dance floors, live music venues, cultural performances, and casinos and gaming establishments.

Bars and Pubs

Beirut has a wide variety of bars and pubs that serve a wide range of patrons. The city offers something for every mood, whether you're looking for a hip place to enjoy handmade cocktails or a relaxed setting to relax with friends.

The bar scenes of Mar Mikhael and Gemmayze are particularly lively, with a wide selection of pubs, cocktail lounges, and rooftop bars. Both locals and visitors like these spots, which fosters a spirit of celebration and friendship.

Beirut's bars are not just places to enjoy a drink; they are also hubs of creativity and art. Many bars host live music performances, art exhibitions, and themed events, making them ideal spots to immerse yourself in Beirut's cultural and social scene.

Nightclubs and Dance Floors

Nightclubs in Beirut are known for their vibrancy and enthusiasm, providing partygoers with an unforgettable experience. The vibrant music culture in the city features a wide range of genres, such as Middle Eastern beats, R&B, hip-hop, and electronic dance music.

Beirut's clubbing scene is opulent, with world-class sound systems, captivating light shows, and well-known DJs spinning tunes till the wee hours of the morning. Beirut's top nightclubs frequently host world-class DJs and foreign guest performers, making every night out a unique experience.

Some of the most well-liked nightclubs in the city are located in Gemmayze, Hamra, and the hip Downtown neighborhood. Here, locals and tourists alike congregate to dance the night away.

Live Music Venues

Beirut provides a wide variety of live music venues that feature both local and international performers for music lovers. Live music in the city is varied, with acts playing jazz, blues, rock, and traditional Lebanese music, among other genres.

Jazz lovers will find solace in the numerous jazz bars scattered throughout the city. These venues create an intimate setting where you can enjoy soulful performances by talented musicians.

Another feature of Beirut's entertainment calendar are music festivals. Music enthusiasts go from near and far to attend events like the Beirut Jazz Festival, Beiteddine Festival, and Batroun International Festival because they provide an opportunity to see top-notch performances against breathtaking scenery.

Cultural Performances

With a plethora of events celebrating art, theater, and dance, Beirut boasts a vibrant cultural environment. A renowned cultural relic, the Beirut Opera House presents everything from modern dance and theatrical plays to traditional operas and ballets.

Renowned locations for art shows, movie screenings, and exhibitions are the Sursock Museum and the Beirut Art Center. These establishments offer guests an insight into Lebanon's rich artistic legacy and modern cultural manifestations.

A trip to one of the city's supper theaters is essential for anyone interested in traditional Lebanese dance and culture. These locations provide an immersive cultural experience by combining a colorful dance show with a delectable Lebanese feast.

Casino and Gaming

For those seeking excitement and the thrill of gaming, Beirut's casinos offer a luxurious and sophisticated experience. The city is home to several world-class casinos that feature a wide array of table games, slot machines, and poker rooms.

The casinos are more than simply places to play games; they frequently feature entertainment events including live music concerts, themed parties, and foreign shows. From the casino floors, guests may take in expansive views of the metropolitan skyline, exquisite dining experiences, and sophisticated bars.

Guests can enjoy gambling and entertainment late into the night at the city's casinos, which are open until the wee hours of the morning.

In conclusion, Beirut's entertainment and nightlife scenes serve as a tribute to the vibrant and international nature of the city. From chic pubs and exciting clubs to enthralling live music venues, cultural events, and opulent casinos, Beirut has a wide variety of experiences to suit every taste. Whether you're looking for a night of dancing, cultural exploration, musical magic, or exhilarating gaming, Beirut's dynamic after-dark events guarantee a memorable and exciting experience that will leave guests with lifelong memories. The city welcomes you to take in its cultural diversity and partake in the celebration of life that characterizes this alluring metropolis as it comes to life after dusk.

CHAPTER SEVEN:
Outdoor Activities and Adventures in Beirut

Beyond its busy cityscape and diverse cultural attractions, Beirut offers a wealth of outdoor experiences that let tourists fully immerse themselves in Lebanon's scenic landscape and spirit of adventure. Beirut offers an abundance of outdoor exploration choices, ranging from exhilarating water sports and calm beaches to energetic hiking routes and intriguing waterfront activities. We'll explore some of the best outdoor pursuits and adventures in Beirut in this chapter, such as waterfront pursuits, hiking and nature trails, beaches and water sports, day visits to neighboring locations, and the thrilling thrill of paragliding above Jounieh Bay.

Waterfront Activities

The Mediterranean Sea fronting Beirut's magnificent waterfront makes for an excellent venue for a variety of outdoor pursuits. Walking, running, and cycling are common activities on the picturesque promenade known as the Corniche, which runs along the coastline and provides stunning views of the sea and the skyline of the city.

Take a boat tour for a leisurely experience to discover the coastline beauties and enjoy the expansive views of Beirut from the water. A lot of boat tours provide fishing expeditions, sunset cruises, and sightseeing excursions, making it the perfect way to take in the gorgeous scenery and sea breeze of the city.

Hiking and Nature Trails

Due to its varied geography, Lebanon has an abundance of hiking and nature paths. Beirut serves as a starting point for a number of scenic hikes suitable for hikers of all skill levels. A beautiful backdrop for a variety of trekking experiences, the neighboring Lebanese Mountains provide an opportunity to get in touch with nature and take in visually amazing landscapes.

Home to ancient cedar trees and a variety of species, the Chouf Cedar Reserve is one of the most well-liked trekking locations in the Beirut area. The reserve is a great place for nature lovers and birdwatchers, with well-marked trails leading to breathtaking overlooks.

Beaches and Water Sports

Beirut's coastline is adorned with beautiful beaches that invite visitors to bask in the Mediterranean sun and enjoy a variety of water sports. Ramlet el-Baida Beach, the largest public beach in Beirut, is a favorite spot for locals and tourists alike, offering soft sandy shores and clear waters for swimming.

For water sports enthusiasts, numerous beach clubs and resorts provide activities like jet skiing, paddleboarding, and parasailing, ensuring a fun-filled day at the beach.

Day Trips to Surrounding Areas

Due to its strategic location, Beirut is a great place to begin day trips to visit the neighboring regions. You can find natural wonders, ancient attractions, and quaint towns only a short drive from the city.

A popular day trip destination is Byblos (Jbeil), one of the oldest continuously inhabited cities in the world. The ancient port city boasts a well-preserved Crusader castle, ancient ruins, and a charming old town with cobbled streets and souks.

The Jeita Grotto, a collection of breathtaking limestone caverns situated north of Beirut, is another must-see location. The grotto provides guided boat trips that take visitors through its breathtaking chambers and underground rivers, making it a weird and unique experience.

Paragliding Over Jounieh Bay

Paragliding over Jounieh Bay is an exciting experience that gives bird's-eye views of the stunning coastline for thrill-lovers and adventure seekers. From Beirut, it takes a short car ride to reach Harissa, a mountainous region featuring paragliding launch spots.

Participants are strapped into a tandem paraglider with an experienced pilot and take off from the mountainside, flying high over the bay, following a quick safety briefing. Through the experience, travelers can feel like they are flying while taking in breathtaking views over the Mediterranean Sea and the surrounding area.

In conclusion, Beirut's outdoor pursuits and excursions provide a variety of unique experiences that highlight Lebanon's scenic landscape and leisure options. Beirut has something for everyone looking for an outdoor vacation, whether they like to explore the coastline, go on strenuous hikes, enjoy the beaches and water sports, go on day trips to discover the neighboring locations, or paraglide. Discover the city's distinct fusion of natural beauties and urban charm, which invites visitors to enjoy a wide range of outdoor experiences and make lifelong memories amidst the glories of nature. Beirut offers countless chances for discovery and excitement, making for a remarkable trip into the heart of Lebanon's magnificent countryside.

CHAPTER EIGHT:
Beirut's Arts and Cultural Scene

Beirut, a city with a rich history and a vibrant present, is a cultural melting pot that embraces a diverse array of arts and cultural expressions. Beirut's cultural landscape is a vibrant tapestry that captures the essence of the city, ranging from top-notch museums and galleries to enthralling theaters for performing arts, modern art spaces, and vibrant cultural festivals. We will delve into the many layers of Beirut's arts and culture landscape in this chapter, covering its museums and galleries, theaters and performing arts, contemporary art spaces, cultural festivals and events, and the exotic realm of Arabic calligraphy and traditional arts.

Museums and Galleries

A remarkable array of museums and galleries showcasing works from different artistic genres and historical periods contribute to Beirut's cultural heritage. Since it sheds light on Lebanon's historical past, the National Museum of Beirut is a veritable gold mine of archaeological marvels.

The Sursock Museum is another iconic institution, housed in a 19th-century mansion, showcasing modern and contemporary art from Lebanon and the Arab world. The museum's diverse exhibitions and art installations offer an immersive experience into the region's contemporary art landscape.

Apart from the large museums, Beirut has a large number of private galleries that display the creations of both established and up-and-coming artists. These galleries support the art culture in the city, which is booming and features anything from conventional painting and sculpture to experimental multimedia pieces.

Performing Arts and Theaters

The performing arts scene in Beirut is vibrant, with several different theaters, concert halls, and performance spaces hosting engaging productions and performances. One of the most well-known outdoor performance spaces in the world is the UNESCO-listed Beirut Hippodrome, a former military installation that today hosts theater productions, music festivals, and concerts beneath the stars.

Established in 1994, the Al-Madina Theater is a significant cultural icon that is essential to the performing arts landscape in Lebanon. The theater promotes creativity and artistic expression by hosting a variety of shows, such as plays, dance performances, and musical concerts.

Contemporary Art Spaces

The numerous art galleries and cultural institutions in Beirut are vital to the city's contemporary art scene, providing a venue for both domestic and foreign artists to exhibit and explore. Zico House is a multifunctional art space located in Gemmayze. It serves as a center for cultural events, seminars, and exhibitions that encourage artistic involvement and dialogue.

The mission of the autonomous contemporary art organization Ashkal Alwan is to promote innovative and critical artistic endeavors throughout the Arab world, including Lebanon. The association has a wide range of activities, such as exhibitions, public events, and residencies, and it has a major impact on the development of contemporary art in Beirut.

Cultural Festivals and Events

Beirut's cultural calendar is jam-packed with colorful festivals and events honoring the city's rich artistic legacy. One of Lebanon's most prominent cultural events, the Beiteddine Festival takes place in the Chouf Mountains every year and draws both local and foreign performers for everything from ballet and theater to classical music.

Another highlight is the Beirut International Film Festival, which offers a wide range of foreign and Lebanese films and gives filmmakers a stage on which to interact with viewers and display their craft.

Some cultural festivals honor particular genres of art; one such event is Beirut Art Week, which honors contemporary art around the city with performances, exhibitions, and public installations.

Arabic Calligraphy and Traditional Arts

Beirut's cultural heritage includes Arabic calligraphy, an age-old art form that honors the beauty of Arabic lettering. Calligraphy covers different areas in the city, demonstrating the artistic prowess and cultural relevance of this traditional art form. Examples of these spaces include vivid street art and exquisite mosque decorations.

Lebanon's traditional arts, such as pottery, ceramics, weaving, and metalwork, are preserved and celebrated through various craft workshops and cultural centers. These traditional arts are passed down through generations, reflecting the country's cultural heritage and craftsmanship.

In conclusion, Beirut's cultural and artistic landscape is a dynamic tapestry that combines modern artistic expressions with the city's ancient heritage. Lebanon's vibrant modern art scene and its ancient heritage are both glimpsed in the city's museums and galleries. Artists have a platform to showcase their skills and interact with a wide range of audiences through performing arts theaters and cultural events. In the meantime, Beirut's modern art venues support experimentation and originality, enhancing the artistic life of the city. Arabic calligraphy and traditional arts showcase the nation's rich heritage and workmanship, while cultural festivals and events provide Beirut's cultural landscape a sense of celebration and unification. Being a melting pot of cultures, Beirut welcomes guests to immerse themselves in the dynamic arts and cultural offerings, turning their trip into a festival of expression, creativity, and the essence of Lebanon's cultural character.

CHAPTER NINE:
Hidden Gems and
Off-the-Beaten-Path in Beirut

Adventuresome travelers can uncover a plethora of hidden jewels and off-the-beaten-path experiences in Beirut, despite the city being well-known for its bustling nightlife and cultural attractions. By showcasing local handiwork in craft stores and artisan workshops, as well as through cozy cafes and rooftop bars with panoramic views, Beirut's hidden jewels provide a distinct and genuine viewpoint of the city. This chapter will cover some of Beirut's lesser-known gems, such as its quaint cafes and rooftop bars, artisan shops and workshops, lesser-known historical sites, oddball and quirky attractions, and tranquil parks and gardens that offer a delightful diversion from the city's bustle.

Cozy Cafes and Rooftop Bars

In the middle of Beirut's bustling downtown, quaint cafes and rooftop bars provide peaceful retreats with stunning views. Beirut is a city that is proud of its coffee culture and is home to several little cafés that offer great coffee along with a cozy atmosphere. These cafes are ideal for relaxing afternoons since they frequently have distinctive décor, live music events, and bookshelves stocked with a wide variety of literature.

Rooftop bars in Beirut are undiscovered treasures that are well worth discovering for anyone looking for stunning views of the city skyline. These bars, perched atop buildings, provide expansive views of the streets below, the mountains, and the Mediterranean Sea. A unique experience that perfectly captures the allure of Beirut's nightlife is sipping drinks while taking in the sunset from a rooftop bar.

Artisan Workshops and Craft Stores

The hidden gems of Beirut are its artisan workshops and craft boutiques, which honor the nation's creative and traditional workmanship. Explore the quiet workshops off the main streets to find talented artists working on one-of-a-kind, handcrafted goods.

Lebanese craftsmen employ a wide range of materials in their work, including jewelry, textiles, glass, ceramics, and pottery. Attending these workshops offers the chance to see the creation process in action and buy unique mementos that honor Lebanon's rich cultural past.

Lesser-Known Historical Sites

Although Beirut's most famous historical sites draw a lot of tourists, the city also has a number of lesser-known historical landmarks that provide a window into its colorful history. Situated within contemporary structures, these obscure historical gems frequently remain undiscovered, awaiting the exploration of inquisitive voyagers.

The Roman Cardo Maximus, an old Roman thoroughfare in Downtown Beirut, is one such location. This undiscovered treasure provides a window into the Roman history of the city and a chance to experience life as it was for ancient cultures.

The majestic St. George Maronite Cathedral, with its breathtaking architecture and exquisite artwork, is another lesser-known historical treasure. This undiscovered treasure offers a calm and reflective area apart from the busy metropolis.

Quirky and Unusual Attractions

There are a number of odd and eccentric attractions in Beirut that give the city's personality a whimsical touch. Soap Museum: A quaint little museum about the history and making of traditional soap in Lebanon is one of these attractions. The museum provides a fascinating look into the skill and artistry involved in producing soap.

The Alice Mogabgab Gallery & Bookstore is another quirky destination worth visiting. This unique space combines an art gallery with a bookstore, creating an ambiance that celebrates creativity and literature.

Serene Gardens and Parks

Beirut's tranquil parks and gardens provide restful havens for recuperation among the city's bustle. In the center of the city, Sanayeh Garden is a peaceful haven with lush meadows, meandering walks, and charming fountains.

A huge urban park that provides a getaway into nature is Horsh Beirut, a hidden treasure. The park offers plenty of room for picnics and leisurely strolls in addition to serving as a sanctuary for a variety of plants and animals.

To sum up, Beirut's off-the-beaten-path adventures and hidden gems provide a fun and genuine tour around the city's lesser-known attractions. While artisan workshops and craft stores offer a chance to learn about the nation's traditional craftsmanship, cozy cafes and rooftop bars offer the ideal places to unwind and take in the expansive views. Discovering lesser-known historical monuments and eccentric attractions offers fresh perspectives on the city's past and a surprising element to the journey. Peaceful parks and gardens provide a much-needed break from the bustle of the city and let tourists re-establish a connection with the natural world amid the busy streets. Travelers will discover the entrancing mysteries and hidden charms that make Beirut an incredibly alluring and mystical place when they stray from the typical route. Discovering these undiscovered treasures ensures a genuine and unforgettable encounter that embodies the essence and vitality of this dynamic metropolis.

CHAPTER TEN:
History and Heritage of Beirut

The vast and diverse heritage of Beirut, a city rich in history, attests to the city's inhabitants' tenacity and the influence of many civilizations. Beirut's historical tapestry is a remarkable tale of religious cohabitation, cultural variety, and post-war restoration efforts, woven together with remnants of Roman and Ottoman civilizations and scars from civil war. This chapter will examine Beirut's history and legacy, covering its role in the American Civil War, Roman and Ottoman influences, archaeological ruins and sites, the city's rich cultural variety, its religious sites, and the amazing post-war reconstruction efforts.

Beirut's Civil War History

The Lebanese Civil War, which raged from 1975 to 1990, was one of the most important episodes in the turbulent past that formed the city's history. Various factions fought for control of the city during this time, wreaking havoc and dividing Beirut.

Certain parts of Beirut still bear the scars of the civil war; bullet-riddled facades and abandoned houses serve as melancholy reminders of the fighting. Nonetheless, Beirut's post-war change and its people's will to rebuild and go on demonstrate the city's resiliency.

Roman and Ottoman Influences

Ancient civilizations that had thrived in the area have also left their mark on Beirut's history. The Roman conquest of the city in the first century BC is among the most important impacts. Beirut, also known as Berytus, flourished as a bustling hub of learning and trade during the Roman era.

In the center of Beirut are Roman ruins, such as the Roman Baths and the Roman Cardo Maximus, which provide insight into the city's prehistoric past.

Following the Roman era, Beirut came under Ottoman rule in the 16th century. The Ottomans left their mark on the city's architecture and urban layout, contributing to the unique blend of historical influences that can still be observed in modern-day Beirut.

Archaeological Sites and Ruins

Beirut's ruins and archaeological sites offer a glimpse into the city's past and demonstrate its rich history. The National Museum of Beirut, as previously said, is home to an extensive collection of objects from many historical periods, including the Phoenician, Roman, Byzantine, and Ottoman periods.

The well-preserved Roman Baths provide tourists with the opportunity to explore historic bathing structures and gain knowledge about the Roman history of the city. A new addition to the city's archaeological riches is the Roman Hippodrome, a site of historic chariot racing.

Cultural Diversity and Religious Sites

Beirut's history demonstrates the city's ability to coexist with several cultures. The city has hosted a number of religious communities over the years, including Druze, Muslims, Christians, and others.

With synagogues, churches, and mosques coexisting side by side, the city's religious sites reflect this diversity. Among the places of worship that epitomize Beirut's inclusiveness are the Maghen Abraham Synagogue, Saint George Maronite Cathedral, and the Mohammad Al-Amin Mosque.

Post-War Reconstruction Efforts

After the civil war ended in 1990, Beirut started an amazing post-war redevelopment process. Large-scale reconstruction efforts were made to repair the damaged cityscape, restore its infrastructure, and revitalize the communities that had been ravaged by the conflict.

Together, architects, urban planners, and legislators redesigned and rebuilt a city that both honored its past and welcomed modernity during the restoration process. The blend of modern and antique architecture in Beirut today is a testament to the city's tenacity and will to recover and prosper.

In summary, Beirut's history and legacy weave a colorful tapestry that depicts the tale of a city molded by many civilizations, wars, and victories. The history of Beirut is one of resiliency, diversity, and cultural complexity, from the remnants of the civil war to the echoes of Roman and Ottoman influences. While the city's religious sites honor its ethos of religious coexistence, its archaeological sites and ruins provide a window into its historical past. The incredible post-war rehabilitation efforts are proof of the Beirutian people's unwavering spirit. Discovering a place where the past and present join forces to create a dynamic and alluring destination that lingers in the hearts of those who experience its distinct charm is what awaits visitors as they delve into the history and legacy of this enchanted city.

CHAPTER ELEVEN:
Insider's Tips and Local Recommendations for Exploring Beirut

When exploring Beirut, delving into the local culture and hidden treasures can enhance your experience and create lasting memories. This chapter will provide insider's tips and local recommendations to help you navigate the city like a true insider. From finding the best places to eat and drink, shopping for authentic souvenirs, mastering transportation, understanding cultural etiquette, to ensuring safety, this guide will equip you with invaluable insights to make the most of your visit to this captivating city.

Where the Locals Eat and Drink

Beirut's culinary scene is a culinary delight, and to enjoy it to the fullest, follow the locals to their favorite eateries and watering holes. For authentic Lebanese cuisine, seek out small family-owned restaurants, often tucked away in side streets and alleys. These places serve delicious and affordable dishes that locals savor daily.

To experience the traditional Lebanese mezze culture, venture to areas like Gemmayze and Mar Mikhael, where you'll find countless restaurants offering an array of small dishes meant for sharing. Don't hesitate to try new dishes and ask the waitstaff for recommendations; they are usually more than happy to help.

For drinks, head to local pubs and bars in the trendy neighborhoods of Hamra and Mar Mikhael. Here, you can mingle with the locals, enjoy a diverse range of beverages, and experience the city's vibrant nightlife.

Shopping for Authentic Souvenirs

When shopping for souvenirs, steer clear of tourist traps and seek out genuine items that showcase Lebanon's exquisite craftsmanship and rich history. To locate distinctive goods created by regional artists, visit local marketplaces and souks such the Souk Ayyas in the Armenian Quarter and the Souk el Tayeb farmers' market.

Seek for artisanal soap and olive oil products, fine pottery, traditional textiles, and handcrafted crafts. You may help local communities and assist in the preservation of Lebanon's cultural history by shopping in these markets.

Transportation and Getting Around

Navigating Beirut's busy streets may seem daunting, but with a few tips, getting around becomes much easier. Walking is one of the best ways to explore the city, as it allows you to immerse yourself in the local culture and discover hidden gems.

Beirut's public transport system offers shared taxis, known as "service" or "van," which are less expensive than ordinary taxis, and buses for longer trips. However, to effectively converse with drivers, you must be familiar with the major thoroughfares and communities.

In Beirut, ride-hailing applications such as Careem and Uber are also accessible, offering a dependable and easy means of transportation within the city, particularly during peak hours.

Language and Cultural Etiquette

The official language of Beirut is Arabic, however many people there also speak French and English, particularly in the tourist districts. Acquiring a few fundamental Arabic phrases can enhance your communication skills and be well-received by the community.

It is crucial for visitors to honor the cultural norms and customs of the area. It's not unusual to receive invitations for meals or coffee because Lebanese people are renowned for their warmth. One excellent method to encounter true

Lebanese warmth and friendliness is to accept these gestures.

Respect worshippers and dress modestly when you attend places of worship. It's also traditional to take off your shoes when visiting someone's house or other specific locations.

Safety Tips and Emergency Contacts

Though, like with any urban region, it's important to exercise caution when visiting Beirut, the city is generally secure for tourists. In busy areas, stay aware of your possessions and refrain from flaunting pricey jewelry or gadgets.

Check with your embassy for any travel advisories or safety updates if you intend to visit less popular destinations.

Dial 112 for general emergencies or 140 for medical crises in case of emergency. Additionally, it's a good idea to have your consulates or embassy's contact details close to hand.

Beirut is a dynamic city that captivates visitors with its distinct fusion of culture, history, and friendliness. You can thoroughly immerse yourself in the spirit of the city and make priceless memories by heeding the advice of locals and insiders. Take pleasure in your exploratory tour around this fascinating place, and allow Beirut's warmth and charm to envelop you as you discover its cultural masterpieces and hidden gems.

CHAPTER TWELVE:
Beyond Beirut: Exploring Lebanon

While Beirut offers a wealth of cultural experiences and treasures, traveling outside the city's boundaries reveals Lebanon's magnificent diversity. Explore Lebanon's stunning assortment of sights, which include natural wonders, historical sites, and ancient ruins. We will explore five amazing locations outside of Beirut in this chapter that highlight the nation's natural wonders, rich history, and cultural legacy: Byblos (Jbeil); Baalbek and the Roman Ruins; Jeita Grotto and Nahr al-Kalb; Chouf Cedar Reserve and Beiteddine Palace; Tyre (Sour) and Sidon (Saida).

Byblos (Jbeil)

Situated to the north of Beirut, Byblos boasts a history spanning over 7,000 years, making it one of the world's oldest continually inhabited cities. Selected as a UNESCO World Heritage Site, the city is known for its ancient remains and Phoenician relics.

Explore the well-preserved archaeological sites of Byblos, such as the Roman Theater, Phoenician Temple, and Crusader Castle. Offering a fascinating fusion of history and local culture, the Old Souk and scenic fishing harbor contribute to the city's attraction.

Baalbek and the Roman Ruins

Get to the breathtaking ancient ruins of Baalbek by traveling to the Beqaa Valley. Baalbek, once known as Heliopolis, was an important religious hub and home to some of the most remarkable Roman temples on the planet.

Two magnificent examples of Roman architecture are the Temple of Bacchus and the Temple of Jupiter, which both include elaborate stone carvings and large columns. For those who love history and architecture, Baalbek is a must-visit location because of its grandeur and historical significance.

Jeita Grotto and Nahr al-Kalb

Just as fascinating as Lebanon's ancient sites are its natural beauties. The Jeita Grotto is a captivating system of limestone caverns decorated with stalactites and stalagmites, located only a short drive from Beirut. Immerse yourself in the stunning magnificence of this underground treasure by exploring the top grotto on foot and the lower grotto by boat.

The Dog River, also known as Nahr al-Kalb, is a fascinating historical site close to Jeita Grotto. It has historical inscriptions and sculptures etched into the cliffs that record the movements of numerous armies and conquerors over time.

Chouf Cedar Reserve and Beiteddine Palace

The stunning Beiteddine Palace and the Chouf Cedar Reserve will captivate both history buffs and nature lovers. As a testament to Lebanon's cultural legacy and environmental preservation efforts, the Chouf region is home to the last remaining cedar forests.

The Beiteddine Palace, a masterpiece of Lebanese architecture, showcases a harmonious fusion of Ottoman, Lebanese, and Italian styles. Its stunning courtyards, ornate interiors, and lush gardens offer a glimpse into the opulence of Lebanon's past rulers.

Tyre (Sour) and Sidon (Saida)

You'll find two coastal cities with a significant cultural heritage further south along the coast. The spectacular Roman Hippodrome and the Al-Bass Archaeological Site are only two of the well-preserved archaeological sites in Tyre, sometimes referred to as Sour in Arabic. Tyre is an ancient Phoenician metropolis.

Another treasure of the coast is Sidon, also known as Saida, which has a quaint old town and important historical sites like the Khan el-Franj and the Crusader Sea Castle. The city's souks provide a chance to discover local customs and purchase one-of-a-kind mementos.

In conclusion, travelers can experience Lebanon's captivating diversity by venturing outside of Beirut. Every place offers a different and engaging experience, from the historical sites of Tyre and Sidon to the natural wonders of Jeita Grotto and Chouf Cedar Reserve. Ancient ruins like those of Byblos and Baalbek are just a few examples. Travelers may fully immerse themselves in Lebanon's rich history, landscape, and culture by going on these trips, making lifelong memories in the process. Whatever your interest—history, wildlife, or culture—Lebanon's hidden gems outside of Beirut will leave you in amazement and yearning to see more of this amazing nation.

CHAPTER THIRTEEN:
Appendix

30 Useful Phrases in Arabic with Pronunciation Guide

1. Hello - Marhaba (mar-ha-ba)

2. Good morning - Sabah al-khair (sa-ba-hal-khayr)

3. Good afternoon - Masa' al-khair (ma-sa-al-khayr)

4. Good evening - Masa' al-noor (ma-sa-al-noor)

5. Thank you - Shukran (shook-ran)

6. You're welcome - Ahlan wa sahlan (ah-lan wa sah-lan)

7. Please - Min fadlak (min fad-lak) - (to a male) / Min fadlik (min fad-leek) - (to a female)

8. Excuse me - Law samaht (law sa-maht) - (to a male) / Law samahti (law sa-mah-tee) - (to a female)

9. Yes - Na'am (na-am)

10. No - La (la)

11. How much? - Bikam? (bee-kam)

12. Where is...? - Ayna...? (ay-na)

13. I don't understand - Ana mish fahim (a-na mish fa-heem)

14. Do you speak English? - Tatakallam inglizi? (ta-ta-kal-lam in-glee-zee)

15. My name is... - Ismi... (ees-mee)

16. What time is it? - Kam as-sa'a? (kam as-sa-a)

17. Can you help me? - Mumkin tesaa'dni? (mum-kin te-saad-nee)

18. I need a taxi - BeHtej taxi (be-h-taj tax-ee)

19. Where is the restroom? - Wayn al-hammam? (wayn al-ham-mam)

20. Cheers! - Fe sahetak (fe sa-heh-tak)

21. Excuse me, can I take a photo? - Law samaht, mumkin swaret souwara? (law sa-maht, mum-kin sa-wa-ret soo-wa-ra)

22. No problem - Ma'alesh (ma-a-lesh)

23. I love Lebanon - Ana bahebak Lebnan (a-na ba-he-bak Leb-nan)

24. Goodbye - Ma'a salama (ma-a sa-la-ma)

25. Have a nice day - Yom sa'id (yom sa-eed)

26. Delicious - Lazeez (la-zez)

27. Can I have the check, please? - Min fadlak, momken el hisab? (min fad-lak, mom-ken el he-sab)

28. Where can I find a pharmacy? - Wayn mumkin ansaj shifaa? (wayn mum-kin an-saj shee-fa)

29. I'm lost - TawA'et (ta-wa-et)

30. Help! - 3awwenni (3aw-wen-nee)

Currency Conversion Chart

1 USD (United States Dollar) ≈ 1500 LBP (Lebanese Pound)

1 EUR (Euro) ≈ 1700 LBP (Lebanese Pound)

1 GBP (British Pound) ≈ 2000 LBP (Lebanese Pound)

1 AED (United Arab Emirates Dirham) ≈ 400 LBP (Lebanese Pound)

1 SAR (Saudi Riyal) ≈ 400 LBP (Lebanese Pound)

(Note: *Exchange rates are approximate and subject to change)*

Packing List for Beirut

- Lightweight and breathable clothing suitable for the Mediterranean climate

- Comfortable walking shoes for exploring the city
- Sunscreen, sunglasses, and a hat for protection from the sun
- Electrical adapter (Lebanon uses Type C and Type D sockets)
- Travel-sized first aid kit and any necessary medications
- Swimsuit and beach towel for beach visits
- Daypack for carrying essentials during excursions
- Lightweight rain jacket or umbrella for unexpected rain showers
- Arabic phrasebook or language translation app
- Reusable water bottle to stay hydrated
- Camera and extra memory cards to capture memories
- Power bank for keeping your devices charged on the go

- Local SIM card or an international roaming plan for mobile connectivity

Hand-picked Hotel Recommendations for Every Budget

Luxury Hotels:

1. Four Seasons Hotel Beirut: Located in Downtown Beirut, offering luxurious amenities and stunning views of the Mediterranean Sea.

2. Le Gray Beirut: A boutique hotel in the heart of the city, featuring modern design and excellent dining options.

3. Phoenicia Hotel Beirut: An iconic hotel with a rich history, offering elegant rooms and lush gardens.

Mid-Range Hotels:

1. Radisson Blu Hotel Beirut Verdun: Situated in the vibrant Verdun area, offering comfortable rooms and a rooftop pool.

2. The Smallville Hotel: A trendy hotel in Badaro, known for its contemporary design and rooftop bar.

3. O Monot Hotel: A stylish boutique hotel in the heart of Beirut, offering personalized service and chic accommodations.

Budget Hotels:

1. Saifi Urban Gardens: A cozy and budget-friendly option in the trendy Saifi Village, close to art galleries and cafes.

2. Napoleon Hotel: A centrally located budget hotel with comfortable rooms and a friendly atmosphere.

3. Minto Suites: Affordable and well-equipped apartments in the bustling Hamra neighborhood.

These hand-picked hotel recommendations cater to various budgets and offer comfortable accommodations in convenient locations, ensuring a pleasant stay during your visit to Beirut. Remember to book in advance, especially during peak travel seasons, to secure the best rates and availability.

As you venture beyond Beirut, explore the local customs and hidden gems while embracing the beauty and diversity that Lebanon has to offer. Safe travels and may your journey be filled with unforgettable experiences and cherished memories.

MAP OF BEIRUT

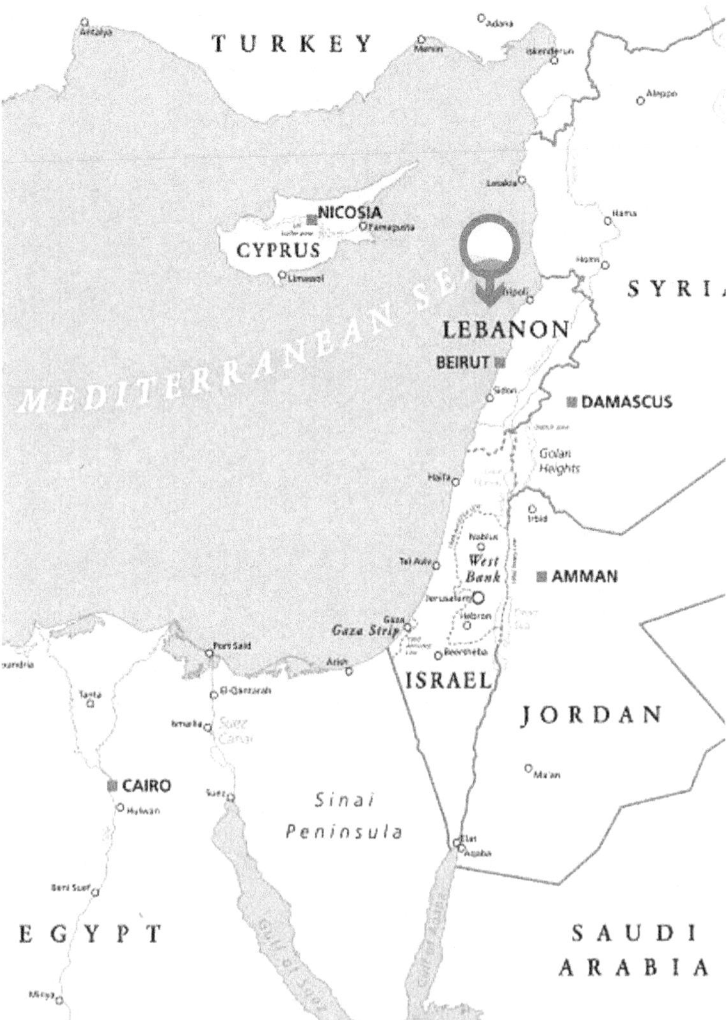

Printed in Great Britain
by Amazon

26203666R00069